God ⬡ grant me the serenity ⬡
to accept ⬡ the things I cannot change,
the courage ⬡ to change the things I can,
and the wisdom ⬡ to know the difference.

Also by Ralph H. Blum

The Book of Runes Tenth Anniversary Edition
Rune Play
The RuneCards

Also by Ralph H. Blum & Susan Loughan

The Healing Runes

the SERENITY RUNES

Five Keys to the Serenity Prayer

Commentary by

RALPH H. BLUM

SUSAN LOUGHAN • BRONWYN E. JONES

ST. MARTIN'S PRESS ❧ NEW YORK

ISBN 0-312-19329-7

First Edition: November 1998

10 9 8 7 6 5 4 3 2 1

DEDICATION

*This book is offered in gratitude
to the Reverend Reinhold Niebuhr.
With your work and your life,
you reached out to us
over a great distance.*

CONTENTS

INVOCATION

Christ speaks to us of the peace
that passeth understanding:
Peace I leave with you,
My peace I give
unto you: not as the world giveth,
give I unto you. Let not your heart
be troubled, neither let it be afraid.
Take these words and stand them
like so many glowing candles
in the forests of the night.
Listen,
and I will speak to you
about serenity.

—R.H.B.

PREFACE
—Susan Loughan

*The only difference between stumbling blocks
and stepping stones is how we use them.*
—Susan Salisbury Richards

Sometimes in life a moment comes that is unlike all others. A moment holding in it the necessary wisdom to help us accept not only what we cannot change but also—for me—the one thing I had feared the most these past ten years. After losing one child a decade ago, I often worried about the health and future of my daughter, Wende, and prayed daily for her safekeeping. My favorite prayer during those years was the Serenity Prayer—comforting words, strengthening words, and certainly wise counsel for this hard-headed Irish woman.

Three years ago Wende, then twenty-three, was in a car accident that resulted, this past fall, in reconstructive surgery. The surgery went well, but then suddenly, without warning, one side of her body became completely numb. After four months of tests and subsequent hospitalizations, on Christmas Eve we were told that Wende had brain lesions consistent with Multiple Sclerosis. This signal event—a diagnosis that would transform both our lives forever—announced that my relationship to the Serenity Prayer was about to change.

During the day-in, day-out rigors of more tests and consultations, Wende and I often found ourselves laughing through our tears. Although I was physically and emotionally drained, nurses and doctors kept saying to me, "You're so calm and grounded." Friends would remark, "You seem so different." They were right. The words of the Prayer had become my way of life. My seemingly inexhaustible supply of spiritual strength was only possible because

I was no longer fighting life's experiences. After twenty years of healing and Twelve Step programs, years of holding sacred the Serenity Prayer, I was finally *living* it.

Although I had known for some time the importance of being grateful for the tests of courage that life brings, I now understood to what extent living the words "the courage to change the things I can" really does strengthen one's soul. Peace and true serenity were finally mine on the eve of Christ's birth.

I want to dedicate my work on this book to my daughter, Wende Williams: It is in your courage and in your love that I see God's wisdom manifest.

INTRODUCTION
—Ralph H. Blum

> *With wisdom comes the knowledge*
> *that the only person I can change is me.*
> — Robert Lee O'Hare

In the past, any real growth in my life always seemed to be fueled by crisis. Back in the late 1970s, my Connecticut farm house had to catch on fire twice before I got the message, decided to sell, and agreed to end my first marriage. These days, however, I am learning to respond to the pressure for growth before the needle gets permanently stuck in the red.

One of the ways I heal and grow is by writing. Working on *The Healing Runes* with Susan Loughan in 1994 brought on a new surge of growth. My wife Jeanne and I had been together four years and our marriage was demanding that I confront and deal with issues of addiction, physical healing and verbal abuse. Writing *The Healing Runes* with Susan introduced me to Twelve Step work, and reintroduced me to the Serenity Prayer, whose five elements—God, Serenity, Acceptance, Courage and Wisdom—are to be found among the twenty-five Healing Runes.

These days when my life feels most unmanageable, when the past becomes a litany of blame and guilt and the future a stormfront of fear, the Serenity Prayer buoys me up with its quiet common sense. What I am learning is quite simple: *All we have is the present. There is no other place where change can occur. The only person I can change is me.*

Let nothing disturb thee,
Nothing affright thee;
All things are passing;
God never changes;
Patient endurance
Attains to all things;
Who God possesses
Is wanting in nothing;
God alone suffices.

—St. Teresa of Avila

1

Pastor Niebuhr's Prayer

God, give us the serenity to accept what cannot be changed,
Give us the courage to change what should be changed,
Give us the wisdom to distinguish one from the other.
—Reinhold Niebuhr

This book is dedicated to Reinhold Niebuhr and it is written to honor the Serenity Prayer, even as we learn to live it. Sometimes the writing has been so effortless that it felt like a meditation on the Prayer. At other times, it seemed as though we were confronted with a great boulder inside of which a stone Buddha was waiting to emerge.

I remember the words of my friend, Rose Boyle: "Just bow to the

Serenity Prayer, and it will transform you. Surrender all control, dare to walk through the door." Bow to it, yes, out of respect. But even as you bow, speak the Prayer, live the Prayer, *be* the Prayer. That is what Reinhold Niebuhr intended.

So many of us were taught that prayer meant asking God for something we wanted or needed. We were also taught to use prayer as a way of thanking God and expressing our gratitude for what we had already received. Yet the very act of prayer, whether silent or spoken aloud, is also a means of opening ourselves to the presence of God in our lives. And it is in that open place—where all worry and care drop away and we are able to listen, truly listen—that we come to appreciate the power of serenity.

I have a deep affection for the Serenity Prayer—the simplicity of it, the way it encourages self-acceptance, the moderation and balance inherent in its words, the grace with which it fosters healing and sobriety. I count the Serenity Prayer as one of the abiding blessings in my life.

Until quite recently, however, I was unaware of the Prayer's source. Somehow I took for granted that its author must be someone like St. Francis of Assisi, inspired on an autumn afternoon, centuries ago in a monastery garden in medieval Umbria.

So I was rather surprised to learn that the Prayer had been adapted from the words of a Yale-trained American theologian, Reinhold Niebuhr (1892-1971) who, in the 1920s, ministered to working people at Detroit's Bethel Evangelical Church, and involved himself in radical labor politics. Later, when he moved to Union Theological Seminary in New York, he maintained his passion for "the social gospel," concerning himself with building "mutual trust and tissues of community," values also to be found at the heart of Alcoholics Anonymous.

By the time Niebuhr published the Prayer in February, 1951, the USO had already distributed it to hundreds of thousands of American servicemen and women during World War II. After the war it was adopted as the Program Prayer by Alcoholics Anonymous and, curiously enough, as the "official motto" of the West German Army Academy. In 1962, the Prayer became Niebuhr's legally when Hallmark Cards paid him for the rights and applied for a copyright in his name.

To this day, however, the origin of the Serenity Prayer has not been clearly established. There is even a possibility that the Prayer, or something very similar, was composed by an 18th century German theologian, Friedrick Oetinger, who wrote under the name of Theodor Wilhelm. In his last years, Niebuhr himself began to wonder whether the Prayer might actually have been something his father, a Lutheran minister, had prayed when Reinhold was a boy.

In the end, however, all that really matters is the abiding truth of the words. Like folk wisdom, the Serenity Prayer, in one form or another, may have been around for a very long time. May it continue to serve generations to come.

God be in my head, and in my understanding;
God be in my eyes, and in my looking;
God be in my mouth, and in my speaking;
God be in my heart, and in my thinking;
God be at my end, and at my departing.

—*Sarum Primer*

2

A Brief History of the Runes

Remarkable. An alphabet that reads A, B, C, D, X, Y, God.
—Margaret Mead, Anthropologist

It is difficult in this day and age to imagine such a thing as a sacred alphabet. I remember my surprise when I first discovered that the Runes belong to an ancient tradition, a tradition whose roots embrace scripture itself. In fact, the Gothic word *runa*, meaning a "mystery," was employed by the Bishop Wulfila in his fourth century translation of the New Testament, when he rendered "the mystery of the kingdom of God" (Mark 4:11) using *runa* for that "mystery."

Working with the Runes carries us back to a time when our ancestors first possessed a written alphabet, and provides us with a hint of how our modern alphabet was formed. Consider, for example, the arrow form frequently found among European petroglyphs dating from the second Bronze Age (1,300 BC). A thousand years later, that same symbol occurs in the first runic alphabet as *teiwaz* ↑—a letter often painted on warriors' shields—whose meaning was "victory in battle." We will never know at what moment the flanges of the arrow were raised, transforming this symbol of strength and victory into our modern letter "T."

By the fourth century AD, the Runes had spread across northern Europe, carried from place to place by warriors, traders, and even by Anglo-Saxon missionaries. For this to happen, a common alphabet was required. This earliest runic alphabet, found among the Germanic tribal peoples, was derived from Latin and Etruscan roots, had twenty-four letters, and was known as the "Elder

Futhark." From the ninth through the twelfth centuries, the Norsemen introduced their runic alphabet into Britain, Iceland, Russia, and wherever their long voyages took them.

Used in commerce and trade, for writing poetry, and for recording the Norse sagas, the Runes were also carved into huge stone memorials erected to Vikings fallen in battle, stones that can still be seen today at a thousand crossroads in rural Sweden. During the 1500 years that Runes were employed in western Europe, they were also linked to religious beliefs and practices. In this sacred function, the runic alphabet served the Germanic and Norse peoples as a means to know the will of the Divine in their lives.

Today we teach our children how letters link with other letters to form words, at which point meaning is present. In ancient times each runic symbol possessed a name, a sound, and most important, a rich cluster of associated meanings. A priest using the Rune *raido* in ceremony, knew that ℝ signified riding or traveling, a journey, or the method of traveling itself. At the highest level of meaning, *raido* evoked the journey made by the soul after death.

This alphabet of twenty-four letters, plus one blank Rune ⬚ —a later intrusion representing the Divine)—forms the basis for our contemporary adaptations of the Runes. The interpretations for the five Serenity Runes found in this book were taken from *The Healing Runes* (St. Martin's Press, 1995). Written to support the emotional and physical healing of those who are in recovery from addiction or abuse, facing a critical illness or preparing for death, *The Healing Runes* evolved from *The Book of Runes* (St. Martin's Press, 1982). In each of these variations, the purpose of the Runes is to serve as a compass for conduct, a guide to right action in the world.

For those of you who come from rigorous religious traditions, know that the Runes will do you no harm. Rather than interfere between you and your Higher Power, they can serve as a mirror in which to glimpse God's purpose and design unfolding in your life.

It is with this sacred aspect of the Runes, and the way in which they serve to illuminate the Serenity Prayer, that this book is concerned. To quote the Benedictine theologian, Father Bede Griffiths, "You could say the Runes are just another means of calling home."

Better a handful of quietness
than both hands full with toil
and much chasing the wind.
—Ecclesiastes

3

MEDITATIONS & TECHNIQUES

There is no need for temples; no need for complicated philosophy.
Our own heart is our temple; the philosophy is kindness.
—The 14th Dalai Lama of Tibet

Absolute attention is prayer.
—Zen Buddhist Saying

Over the years, Reinhold Neibuhr's words have become so widely known that millions now take comfort from them in their yearning for the blessings of serenity and for all that the Prayer imparts. Truly it is a prayer for all God's people, in all seasons and in all situations.

This book is meant to serve as an aid to meditation. While we were writing, we began each day by speaking the Prayer aloud. Performing this simple act became our way of inviting serenity into our lives, and making its presence felt in our words and in our actions.

Weaving the Runes into the words of the Prayer gave us an opportunity to consider, with new eyes, each of the Prayer's four facets—Serenity, Acceptance, Courage and Wisdom—and the ways in which their light is focused through the lens of the Divine. You might say that the Prayer provided the themes, and we created variations on them, the way one musician composes variations on the themes of another.

Among the benefits we received through practicing these exercises was the way in which they helped us to stop and really consider the meaning of the Prayer. Helped us, in fact, to speak the

Serenity Prayer with serenity. However you use these exercises—to begin your day, with your children or your partner, before an important meeting, or in moments of crisis—as time goes by, you will find yourself dwelling more and more in the peace of the Prayer.

HOW TO USE THE SERENITY RUNES

Begin by repeating the words of the Prayer, either out loud or to yourself. Next pick a Serenity Rune from your bag. Now, turn to that Rune's interpretation at the back of the book and let it serve as a meditation on the aspect of the Prayer that is calling for your attention: your relationship with God, Serenity, Acceptance, Courage or Wisdom. Let the words guide you in the moment and support you through your day.

God ◯ grant me the serenity ▷...

I'm thinking of a Wednesday afternoon, when it already felt as though the entire week was trashed: missed deadlines, appointments canceled, delays upon delays, until I thought I might explode with frustration. My inner critic had me by the throat and was blaming me for tardiness, lack of focus, and wasted opportunities. At which point, through the Internet, came the following thread of E-mail wisdom: *The late worm does not get eaten by the early bird.*

I suddenly realized that I hadn't had a good laugh all week and felt myself relax. As it turned out, things I thought I had lost out on proved to be better avoided. When I heard what had happened at a meeting I missed, I was glad to have been absent and experienced, yet again, serenity's embrace.

As one friend says, "Do your best to keep the momentarily

momentous from disrupting your serenity. What works for me is to spend a moment in gratitude to God, while remembering all those people who helped me get to where I am today."

THE DAILY RUNE OF SERENITY

It is my practice to start the day by speaking the Serenity Prayer out loud and pausing at the end of each line to consider how that part of the Prayer applies to my life right now. The following is an example of how I used the Daily Rune while writing this book:

God grant me the serenity . . .
I take a deep breath and let go of everything, all thoughts, all worries, all concern for the future.

To accept the things I cannot change . . .
The deadline rushing toward me when this manuscript will be due on our editor's desk.

The courage to change the things I can…
Knowing that my creative flow dries up in the presence of fear, my challenge is to continue working as though there were all the time in the world, allowing the deadline to provide support and energy for the task, even as it urges me on to the finish line.

And the wisdom to know the difference…
I look at the things that call for my attention, ranging from what can be done this day, to traits of character, to my skills as a partner and husband. Whatever the case may be, with a quiet mind I can more easily find the wisdom to distinguish the call for courage from the need for acceptance, always remembering that the only thing I can ever really change is me.

Next I draw one of the five Runes from my bag to discover which aspect of serenity I need to live most mindfully this day. To complete my meditation, I read the interpretation from the back of the book, paying particular attention to those words or phrases that seem to jump off the page. Sometimes I write about the Rune I chose in my journal, usually I say the name of the Rune out loud. Another time I might put it in my pocket and carry it with me for the rest of the day, as a kind of touchstone, a reminder to embody that aspect of serenity.

A MANTRA FOR SERENITY

A mantra is a word or phrase which, when repeated either silently or aloud, is believed to help us open to the Will of the Divine. For some people, chanting the timeless sound *Om* brings them to a place of calm. My favorite is the ancient Aramaic prayer *Maranatha* which means, "Come, Lord." I find that when I repeat the word "Ma-ra-na-tha," throughout the day, I feel more peaceful inside, no matter what is happening around me. Another of my favorites is the simple affirmation, *I will to will Thy Will*. Then there are days when I repeat, "God is with me … God is with me … " over and over again. *Keep it simple* makes a perfect mantra, as does *One day at a time*.

Certain words seem to possess the power to ease a troubled spirit. Rarely does a day go by that I don't invoke the Serenity Prayer. You could hardly ask for a better mantra.

ON TAKING A PRAYER BREAK

There are times when I hear myself say, "I'm sorry, I simply lost it." And yet, lost what? My composure? My good sense? Usually it is my peace of mind. At other times, I have the feeling that I am losing my center, that I am out of balance, incapable of acting from a place of reason, from a core of clear intention. *Things fall apart/The center does not hold*, so wrote William Butler Yeats. At such difficult moments, I pick a Rune to help me get in touch with my feelings and my center.

When you find yourself feeling wobbly or out of sync, take a prayer break. Pick a Rune to help reconnect you to your Source and set your feet back on the path that leads you to what you truly are.

To accept ⟨ the things I cannot change . . .

I remember a day two years ago when my serenity was in tatters and energy was leaking away through every pore and with each wasteful thought. Then, in the midst of all my indigestible emotions and judgmental yammering, I somehow entered a place of silence. And from that place I heard a gentle voice saying, *As if it matters… As if it matters…*I took the words to mean that I would do well to leave the future in the hands of the Divine. It seemed to me my wiser self was saying, "Has it ever occurred to you that to worry about the outcome is simply admitting that you mistrust God?"

WHEN THE NEEDLE IS IN THE RED

Do you ever experience moments when all the alarms are going off, collapse threatens, and your life is in danger of boiling over? When the needle is in the red, take whatever steps you can to slow the process down, remembering even as you act, that regardless of the chaos around you, *how you respond to what is happening is entirely within your control*. Then, sit quietly and close your eyes. Use what I call a "circuit breaker." Repeat the Serenity Prayer. Say the Lord's Prayer or the *Gayatri*. Recite the words you love from the Koran or the Talmud or the *Tao Te Ching*. Words worn round and smooth in the river of serenity.

THE GIFT OF SOLITUDE

Take a full day just for yourself and let go of everything that is troubling you. Find the time, make the time to *let go and let God*. If a full day is out of the question, give yourself a few hours during which no one can make any demands on you. Turn off the phones, the radio, the television. Go for a walk by yourself and breathe deeply. Take a hot bath or simply eat a meal in silence. What is essential here is to give yourself the gift of solitude.

MINDFULNESS TRAINING

All you need for this exercise is a bell. You can use your alarm clock, the clock on your computer or the neighborhood church bells—even an egg timer will do. Set the timer so it will ring in one hour. When the alarm goes off, stop whatever you're doing and simply breathe for a moment. Then ask yourself, "What aspect of the Serenity Prayer do I need to focus on right now?" Is it courage? Acceptance? Take a moment to repeat the Prayer and allow its wisdom to speak to you.

If you are out in the world, you can still practice mindfulness.

Waiting at a red light, sitting at the bus stop, or standing in line at the bank—wherever you find yourself—rather than being consumed by impatience, use the time to relax and *live* the Serenity Prayer. With a bit of imagination, you will discover countless ways to weave the Prayer into the fabric of your daily life, and in so doing, bring a quality of peace and serenity to everything you do.

The courage ⤊ *to change the things I can ...*

My profound thanks go to Wanda Gale Logan who provided me with a key to unlock my courage. In confusing or difficult moments, I remind myself that God is right at my side by saying, *God is with me, God is with me, God is with me.* Then, looking around, I do an inventory of God's presence: *God is in the air I breathe, God is in the gray sky, God is in the sidewalk beneath my feet...*until I feel surrounded by God, immersed in God.

While writing this book in New York, I sometimes awoke with

feelings of irrational despair, so I chanted *God is with me, God is with me*, until the despair dissolved. When I was late for a meeting and unable to find a cab, I remembered to begin my inventory right there in the street: *God is in the stop lights, God is in the honking horns, God is in the steam curling from the manhole covers, God is with me, God is with me...* continuing until a taxi stopped to pick me up.

Just saying these words reminds me that God is with me at all times, ready to help me free up my courage and change the things I can.

CHANGE YOUR AUDIO INPUT

Turn off the television or talk radio, unplug the phone, and exchange the hectic demands of the outside world for a CD of soothing sounds—sounds from nature, a choir singing Gregorian chants, pan pipes playing or a Celtic harp—any sounds that open you to feelings of serenity. By changing what you listen to, you can soothe your frazzled nerves and relate to the world with a calm and open heart.

THE YOGA OF GRATITUDE

Sometimes when we feel stuck, unable to find the clarity to take the next step, all we really need to do is make a small shift in our attitude and realize that, in time, this too shall pass. If you can't find the strength to change your attitude, write down ten things for which you are truly grateful. I am always amazed at just how quickly this simple exercise improves my frame of mind.

IMAGINE

It's three in the afternoon, your energy is non-existent, you're facing a deadline, and there's no relief in sight. What you're yearning for is to be anywhere but where you are now. That's when it's time to take a break and give yourself the gift of imagination.

Sit back in your chair, let your answering machine handle the phone, close your eyes and just imagine that you are in your favorite place in nature. See yourself in the mountains, lying on a tropical beach, or paddling a canoe—wherever your imagination takes you. Feel the warmth of the sun on your skin, breathe the fragrant air and listen to the sound of the water. Treating yourself to a few imaginary moments can smooth out your gnarly mood and allow you to return to the task at hand, refreshed and with newfound energy.

CALLING A TIME OUT

When you find yourself in an argument that is going nowhere fast, agree to call a time out. Walk away, actually change your surroundings. At the office take a hike to the water fountain, the supply room, or to the privacy of the bathroom. At home, carry out the garbage, water your plants, or make yourself a cup of tea. And while you're taking your time out, repeat the Serenity Prayer.

Calling a time out doesn't have to be complicated. Once around the block can do the trick. When you return, you will usually find that something in you has shifted.

And the wisdom ⟨ᚱ⟩ *to know the difference.*

New York City. Full Summer. I awoke one Monday morning, went out into the street and saw a battered young woman being led into the 18th Precinct Station. Immediately my mind began asking questions for which I had no answers, so I said a prayer for her well being and continued on my way.

Walking down the crowded Avenue of the Americas, I thought about my life and picked a Rune, asking "Where am I on the path of serenity?" And right there, between my fingers, was the Rune of Wisdom ᛈ, reminding me that "to accept and grow from life's lessons is the beginning of wisdom." New vision, new choices, new paths—that is the progression along wisdom's way.

When you feel that life has no choices to offer you, it is time to pray for wisdom. Call on your experience, on your courage and patience—all your skills and abilities—and bring them to bear on what is happening. Then turn your will and the outcome over to God, and the light of wisdom will show you the way.

As I walked with the crowd, I said another prayer for that young woman, asking that she be held in wisdom's embrace.

HEAVENLY FAXES AND DIVINE E-MAIL

According to my friend, sailor Ben, the Runes function as a message center, a place where we receive "heaven's faxes" and the "divine E-mail" that assist us in making the course adjustments we need in order to navigate the shoals and sandbars of daily life. We can send and we can receive, and sometimes a message is waiting for us when we call home—that place inside ourselves where, more than anything else, we yearn to know and do God's Will.

If you are feeling overwhelmed by a situation that seems too much to handle, take a moment to share your concerns with your Higher Power. Then draw a Serenity Rune and read the words of the interpretation out loud. The counsel you receive will be as clear as an E-mail message glowing on your computer screen.

THE PATH OF SERENITY

Seek out people whose serenity you admire. Talk with them, go to a meeting together, pray with them. That's a way to make a start.

At first you will become aware of a moment of serenity here, a moment there. As time goes by, those moments will flow together, forming pools of serenity. Eventually the pools will merge into a stream that carries you on your way, even when you feel you don't have the strength to move yourself. As you start to experience your own serenity, stay with it, live it, until one day you will realize that serenity has become your way of life.

KEEPING A SERENITY JOURNAL

Keeping a Serenity Journal will provide you with a map of your journey, the swamps and deserts as well as the high plateaus and green valleys. Sometimes the writing will flow effortlessly and be filled with the joy of new discovery. At others, your journal writing may be heavy with pain. Ask yourself: Does addictive behavior run through my family? If so, have some of these same patterns emerged in my life? What steps can I take to change things?

Write about the times you were sure you wouldn't make it and yet you did. Write about what got you through and about the people who supported you in reclaiming your strength. Then draw a

Serenity Rune, read the interpretation, and set down any helpful insights that come to you. Keeping a journal can afford you both a fresh perspective and opportunities to see how much you've grown.

Imagine having a friend to whom you can always tell the truth and express your feelings, knowing you will never be judged or criticized. Journaling can provide you with just such a friend.

Secure in the knowledge that serenity exists, let us all take the steps necessary to change—individually, in our families, our communities, and as a nation. Yet how are we to begin? For some of us Twelve Step work—a process whose rewards are sobriety and serenity—is the answer. For others, the choice may be to open the closed doors to the self, either privately or with the help of a therapist or someone you know and trust. Whatever path beckons, know that, with time, serenity will become your companion and your friend.

So work with the Serenity Runes and repeat the Prayer aloud a thousand times, trusting in the steps you are taking daily. Whatever your chosen path, it is our hope that these exercises will support and comfort you along the way.

If you bring forth what is within you,
*   what you bring forth will save you.*
If you do not bring forth what is within you,
*   what you do not bring forth will destroy you.*
                    —Acts of John, *Gnostic Scripture*

4

RUNE
INTERPRETATIONS

God, the Divine

> *God grant me the serenity*
> *to accept the things I cannot change,*
> *the courage to change the things I can,*
> *and the wisdom to know the difference.*

Divine love is present in every season of the heart. Throughout our lives, that love nurtures us, comforts us, inspires and teaches us and, at the end, calls us home.

When did you first begin to know the Divine? Was it in the innocence of your childhood? Was it through adversity or loss that you began your search? Are you still searching? Or have you always known there was a power greater than yourself guiding your life?

Through all of the world's religions—from temples and churches, mesas and mountain tops—the Divine speaks to us. For some, the Divine dwells only within; for others, God is present everywhere. Consider the poet's call to see God in a blade of grass. How wonderful then, to see God in the face of another human being.

Receiving this Rune is a gentle reminder to open your heart to the presence of God, and listen. For God always speaks when we are ready to hear.

If the night is long, and you are sitting at the bedside of a sick or dying loved one, let the Divine be your strength. If you find yourself facing a challenge for which you feel inadequate and unprepared, or if you are in the season that calls for reconciling your life, remember that acceptance and forgiveness are two of our greatest teachers. What you are is God's gift to you, what you make of yourself is your gift to God.

Our lives are ordered for us by the Divine so that we are never given more than we can handle. Yet if the present problem seems too great, and you are too weary to travel further, bless this moment and turn your life over to God. As you do so, your burden will be lifted and you will find the courage to go on. And remember this: In the life of the Spirit, we are always at the beginning.

However the Divine enters your life—through your work in the world, through your love for a child, or a partner, or for our Mother Earth—God's love is the deepest truth available to us all. Once you have made this truth your own, you need never want, never fear again.

And at the end, it is God who calls us home:

I am the Life and the Light and the Way. The earth is my garden. Each of the souls I plant as seeds germinates and flowers in its season, and in each I am fulfilled. There is no cause for grief when a blossom fades, but only rejoicing for the beauty it held and praise that my will is done and my plan served.

I am one with all creatures and none is ever lost, but only restored to me, having never left me at all. For what is eternal cannot be separated from its source.

Serenity

Receiving this Rune is recognition of how far you have come along the path of healing. Give thanks to God for the blessings serenity brings.

There is a place inside our being where serenity dwells. In the past, we hardly knew this quiet place with its freedom from want and need. Take time each day to nourish yourself with the comfort you will find there, for it is from this place of tranquillity and peace that all service flows. And so we pray:

> *God grant me the serenity*
> *to accept the things I cannot change,*
> *the courage to change the things I can,*
> *and the wisdom to know the difference.*

Honesty leads to serenity and patience issues from it; grief, anger and fear are resolved in its embrace, while trust and faith are nourished by serenity, and love thrives in its presence.

Above all, *remember to live your life one day, one moment at a time*. Through a life lived in serenity, we come to know and understand our closeness to the Divine.

Become familiar with what serenity means in your daily life. Without serenity, wounds are slow to heal, while in its presence, all things are possible. If serenity is absent from your world, and you still find yourself riding the merry-go-round of chaos and denial, ask the Divine for the guidance and the strength to face your life with courage. And if you feel your inner peace slipping away, know that through the power of prayer, God will restore it to you.

The Serenity Prayer is a precious gift containing all the elements of divine healing. When you allow serenity to fill your days and nights, you have truly begun to heal your life.

Acceptance

This is a Rune of major blessings, blessings received and blessings bestowed. Acceptance forms the foundation for loving yourself. As you rebuild your life and come to terms with the past, you will begin to know the serenity that accompanies self-acceptance. For out of that serenity arises the willingness and the courage to greet each new day with a quiet heart. Therefore waste not a moment to invoke the Serenity Prayer:

> *God grant me the serenity*
> *to accept the things I cannot change,*
> *the courage to change the things I can,*
> *and the wisdom to know the difference.*

If something is troubling you, know that the time has come to accept the things you cannot change, especially if they are causing you confusion, pain, or sorrow. And while you may be unable to alter your present situation, what you can do is change your response to that situation. Herein lies your freedom, a freedom that will, in time, permit you to move on.

For it is the gradual acceptance of our feelings and our memories of the past that enables us to change. If you find depression, anger, or resentment blocking your progress, turn to prayer, knowing that through prayer you will find your way to acceptance.

Here is a thought so simple that it might seem trivial, and yet it is the very life blood of acceptance: *Where you are now is exactly where you need to be, and you have a perfect right to be there.* Forgive your imperfections and know that you can set a new course for your life, one degree at a time, one day at a time.

There is a special kind of valor in accepting the truth of what is happening in our lives. And until we do so, how can we possibly teach our children about the power of acceptance—acceptance of themselves, acceptance of the differences between themselves and others? How can we create the possibility for lasting change, or any hope for altering the course of human events in years to come?

Receiving this Rune calls for gladly giving up the old and being content to live, for a time, empty, knowing that what is yours will come to you.

↑ *Courage*

In drawing this Rune you are being asked to recognize and honor the courage and strength of your own spirit. As you do, you will grow in the faith and understanding necessary to continue traveling the road you have chosen, and to face with wisdom whatever challenges life brings. Courage is faith in action.

Anyone who has been sorely tested—lost their livelihood, been critically ill, recovered from addiction, suffered through the death of a loved one, or broken the silence of spousal abuse—knows well the courage it takes to heal, to carry on, or start anew. The insight gained from these transforming experiences gives us hope and reminds us that one of the rewards of courage is wisdom.

Whenever you react to a situation with panic or denial, there is no place for courage to take hold. Are you being asked to make a leap of faith into an uncertain future? If the situation confronting you feels overwhelming, think of the people you know who have faced adversity with grace, and pray for their example to inspire you:

> *God grant me the serenity*
> *to accept the things I cannot change,*
> *the courage to change the things I can,*
> *and the wisdom to know the difference.*

For some, this Rune is a call to risk reaching out and asking for help. For others, it announces that the cycle of sorrow and pain has finally come to an end. If the past still troubles you, know that the past is often healed by a courageous heart and mind.

Time and again, the true test of courage is to live rather than to die, to survive the crisis and continue on the path of healing. Take comfort also from this: There is an intimacy with the Divine that grows out of the small brave steps we take, an intimacy that helps us through each day.

Be at peace, and walk the path of healing with courage. Now it is time to go out into the world and live the life you were born to live.

Wisdom

It has been said that wisdom is a map on which to follow the journey of the spirit, a sacred text of understanding from which to learn about the care of the soul.

The ability to accept and grow from life's lessons is the beginning of wisdom. As wisdom deepens, it lends inspiration to creativity and acceptance to grief. The greatest good, said St. Augustine, is wisdom.

Each time you pick this Rune, take a quiet moment in the midst of the day's occupations and consider the issue at hand. Is it part of the endless coming to be and passing away? Or is it part of that which abides? To recognize the difference is to see with the eyes of wisdom.

Oftentimes when we ask life for answers and there is no immediate answer, God provides us with a new way of seeing. And with this new way of seeing, right choices and true paths reveal themselves.

It is through wisdom that loss becomes a bridge and tragedy becomes a teaching. That is wisdom's way. And love's way. For it is wisdom that teaches the mind to understand and learn through love.

As we grow in wisdom, we learn to seek our counsel and our comfort in the Will of Heaven, and to this end, we pray:

> *God grant me the serenity*
> *to accept the things I cannot change,*
> *the courage to change the things I can,*
> *and the wisdom to know the difference.*

The light of God surrounds me;
The love of God enfolds me;
The power of God protects me;
The presence of God watches over me.
Wherever I am, God is

—Anon

Envoi: In Praise of Change

In prayer, come empty, do nothing.
—St. John of the Cross

Sometimes, when I repeat the Serenity Prayer aloud while reaching into the bag and touching the five smooth stones, I feel the absence of a sixth Rune—a Rune of change.

Change is central to the Prayer's very purpose. If we are the arrows, then change is the bow: "to accept the things I cannot change" and "the courage to change the things I can."

As it happened, last summer, while working with my wife Jeanne on our next project, we found what we had been searching for. The fourteenth Rune ⟨, which began as *Opening* in *The Book of*

Runes, then emerged as *Acceptance* in *The Healing Runes* and *The Serenity Runes,* now revealed itself as the Rune of *Change* on the next turn of the runic wheel, *The Relationship Runes.*

It might be said this way:

At the heart of openness is the need for acceptance—acceptance of ourselves, acceptance of others, and acceptance of the right of all God's creatures to be in the world. Once there is openness and acceptance, self-change becomes a real possibility. We were all born open to life—and open to change. Now it is time to reclaim our birthright.

Make it so for all my relations.

Ralph H. Blum

Acknowledgments

Jeanne Elizabeth Blum, who held the fort, kept the faith and urged us on with her love and common sense.

Deborah Daly, whose designs provide elegant, economical form to the Runes packages.

Tom Dunne, who saw the potential in a small bag of Runes that made this project possible.

Nancy Fox, whose advice, wit, and creative use of discipline have saved many a wayward expedition.

Sally Richardson, for holding the vision and always taking the time to make us laugh.

John Sargent, who sees to it that there's a card of fair play in the deck.

Alan B. Slifka, whose active quest for peaceful coexistence in the world inspires us to do our part.

Mitchell Stein & *Marilee Talman*, who helped us to change some of the things we could.

Janene McGaha Williams & *Rae Lynn Denton*, who first had the insight to give the Serenity Prayer its own little bag of amethyst Runes.

THE RUNEWORKS

The RuneWorks was established in 1983 as a resource for people working with the Viking Runes. We are now especially interested in learning of your experiences with *The Serenity Runes:* How have they served you? Have you any suggestions that might increase their usefulness? Or any ideas for new ways of using them?

If you have difficulty finding *The Serenity Runes* or any of our other books—*The Book of Runes, Rune Play, The RuneCards* or *The Healing Runes*—in your local bookstores, or if you would like to purchase additional copies of these books (with or without stones or cards) through The New Oracle Catalogue, please contact us at:

THE RUNEWORKS
PO Box 1320   Venice CA 90294
1-800-355-RUNE (7863)   bronwyn@runeworks.com

Whether cut into stone or engraved on paper, the function of the Runes remains the same. And so we offer *The Serenity Runes* to novices and veteran users alike. May this book serve you well and, in so doing, enable you to serve the highest good, the Will of the Divine for you in your life.

ABOUT THE AUTHORS

Harvard-trained cultural anthropologist RALPH H. BLUM has been working with the Runes as a tool for self-counseling since 1977. He and his wife, Jeanne Elizabeth, make their home in Haiku, Hawaii.

SUSAN LOUGHAN is a healer and a counselor who specializes in recovery from abuse. Susan and her daughter, Wende Williams, are living in Santa Fe, New Mexico.

BRONWYN E. JONES has been editing and writing about the Runes with Ralph Blum since 1981. She lives in Los Angeles, California and manages The RuneWorks.